QED My Body

My Bones

Sally Hewitt

QED Publishing

Copyright © QED Publishing 2008
First published in the UK in 2008 by
QED Publishing
A Quarto Group company
226 City Road
London EC1V 2TT

www.qed-publishing.co.uk

A catalogue record for this book is
available from the British Library.

ISBN 978 1 84835 040 3

Printed and bound in China

Author Sally Hewitt
Consultant Terry Jennings
Project Editor Judith Millidge
Designer Kim Hall
Picture Researcher Claudia Tate
Illustrator Chris Davidson

Publisher Steve Evans
Creative Director Zeta Davies

Picture credits

Key: t = top, b = bottom, m = middle,
l = left, r = right

Alamy Jim Zuckerman 7, Jupiterimages-Polka Dot 17t
Corbis Jennie Woodcock-Reflections Photolibrary 19r,
Virgo Productions-Zefa 19l
Getty Images Barbara Peacock 17t
Shutterstock Irina Klebanova 5b, Teodor Ostojic 5t,
Elena Elisseeva 6, Roberto Kylio 8, Olga Lyubkina 8,
Julian Rovagnati 8, Kivrins Anatolijs 9b, Graca
Victoria 9t, Philip Lange 10t, Serghei Starus 10b, George
P Choma 11, Ariusz Nawrocki 12, Andresr 13tl, Gelpi 13m,
Kameel4u 13tr, Cindy Minear 14, Jiang Dao Hua 15,
JoLin 21b

Words in **bold** are
explained in the glossary
on page 22.

Contents

What is your skeleton?

Your skeleton is like a strong frame. It gives your body its **shape**, holds you upright and lets you move. It **protects** soft parts of your body such as your heart and lungs.

Your skeleton is made up of **bones** of different shapes and sizes. Each bone has a job to do.

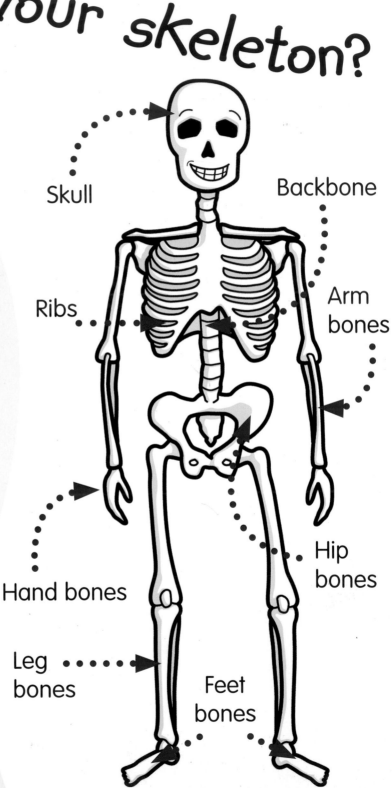

Skull

Backbone

Ribs

Arm bones

Hand bones

Hip bones

Leg bones

Feet bones

Your body is **alive** and growing, and so are your bones. As you grow older, your bones become harder and stronger. By the time you are fully grown, you will have 206 bones.

A baby has tiny hands and feet and soft, bendy bones.

Activity

Which of your bones can you feel through your skin?

Can you feel the top of the bone in your upper arm? Your ribs?

Your bones

Your bones need to be strong and light. Bones are light enough to let you jump and strong enough not to break when you land.

Marrow

Hard bone

Spongy bone

The outside layer of a bone is hard, and the middle layer is like a sponge. In the centre of many bones is a jelly called marrow.

6

Even though bones are very strong, they sometimes break. Bones are amazing! They can mend themselves and become just as strong again.

It usually takes about six weeks for a broken bone to mend.

If you break your arm, you go to hospital. A doctor sets your broken bone, and your arm is put in a plaster cast to hold the bone in place. A sling **supports** your arm while it heals.

7

Healthy bones

Just like the rest of your body, your bones need plenty of good food and **exercise**, as well as rest and sleep.

Milk, eggs, cheese and yogurt, tinned salmon and sardines, as well as leafy, green vegetables all help to keep your bones strong and healthy.

Whatever exercise you enjoy, such as running, dancing or ball games, will keep you active and help your bones to grow strong.

Do something active every day.

Wear a helmet when you ride a bicycle to protect your skull. Wear pads to protect your knees and elbows when you skate.

You can have fun and look after your bones!

9

Joints

Your bones join together at places called **joints**. Most of the joints in your skeleton can move.

If you didn't have joints, you would be as stiff as a statue.

Activity

Move around.
Can you work out which
of your joints move?
What kind of movements
can they make?

Your joints move in different ways. You have 'ball-and-socket' joints, where your arms join your shoulders and where your legs join your hips. These joints let your arms and legs move round in a circle.

Ball-and-socket joint

Elbows and knees are 'hinge' joints. They move backwards and forwards like the hinges on a door.

Your skull

Your skull is made up
of several bones. It is very
strong. Its most important job is
to protect your brain. Feel the shape
of your skull. It has two holes
for your eyes. Your jaw opens
and closes when you
talk and also when
you eat.

The top of your skull
is exactly the right
shape and size to
cover and protect
your brain.

The bones in your skull give your face its shape. We all have a forehead, eyes, nose, a mouth and a chin. Everyone looks just a bit different so we can recognize each other easily.

It would be very confusing if we all looked exactly the same.

Activity

Look in the mirror and draw a picture of your face. Then, draw your friend's face. Which parts of the drawings look the same and which look different?

13

Your backbone

Your backbone, or 'spine', runs right down the middle of your back. It is made up of 26 small bones. If it were made of just one long bone, you would not be able to bend or twist.

Spine

Activity

Bend your knees, curl your back and touch your toes, then stand up again. Feel your backbone bend and straighten up again.

14

Your backbone holds you upright.
If you stand, walk and sit with
a straight back, your spine
supports your whole body.
If you let your back bend
while you are standing or
sitting, you will soon
start to ache all over.

Gymnasts
hold their
backs straight
to help them
balance.

Your ribs

Your ribs are shaped like a cage. They protect your heart, which pumps blood round your body, and your lungs, which you use for breathing.

You have 12 pairs of ribs. They are fixed to your backbone. The top seven pairs of ribs are fixed to your breastbone at the front.

Ribs

Lungs

Breastbone

Heart

16

You can feel your ribs and you can probably see the shape of them through your skin, too.
The bottom two pairs of ribs are only fixed at the back so they can move more easily when you breathe in and out.

Activity

Take a deep breath. Your lungs will fill up with air just like this balloon.

17

Arms and hands

You use your arms and hands to grip and to pick things up, write and draw, and play with toys!

Each arm, wrist and hand is made up of 30 bones, which help you make all these different movements.

Elbow

Arm

Hand

Thumb

Wrist

Fingers

The bone in the top of your arm is strong and thick. You have two thinner bones in the bottom of your arm and 27 bones in your hand and wrist!

Lots of little bones in your fingers help you make small movements.

Activity

Make a model with modelling clay. Notice how you move all the bones in your arms and hands.

Legs and feet

You use your legs to walk, run, jump, stand and sit. The bone in the top of your leg is the longest bone in your body. It is also very strong.

Kneecap

Leg

Ankle

Foot

Toes

A bone called the kneecap protects your knee joint. Children often cut and bruise their knees, so kneecaps have an important job to do!

Have you ever cut or bruised your knee?

It is fun to make footprints on a sandy beach. You can make footprints at home, too!

Activity

Put some dark paper in a tray and sprinkle flour on top of it. Stand in the flour. Now carefully step out without smudging the flour. Can you see how the bones in your foot spread out to help you stand?

Glossary

Alive
You are alive, and so are plants and animals. Things that are alive grow, move, eat and can sense what is going on around them.

Bone
Bones are strong and light. The 206 bones in your body are joined together to make up your skeleton.

Exercise
Exercise is moving about, for example running, swimming, jumping, stretching and skipping. Exercise helps to keep your body strong and healthy.

Joint
'Joint' is the name given to a part of the body where two bones meet. Most of your joints can move. Your elbows and knees are joints.

Protect
'Protect' means to keep something safe from being hurt. Your skull protects your brain.

Shape
Everything has a shape. For example, a ball is a round shape. Your skeleton gives your body its shape.

Support
'Support' means to hold something upright or stop it from falling.

Notes for parents and teachers

1. Have fun drawing a skeleton together. Look at the picture on page 4 to help you. Talk about the shape of the bones you are drawing and feel them under your skin. When you have drawn the skeleton, stick it onto some card and cut it out. Now cut it into sections: head, body, arms and legs. You can put the sections back together using paper fasteners to make a skeleton with a moving head and limbs.

2. Visit a museum with skeletons on display or look at a book with pictures of human, animal or even dinosaur skeletons. Notice that they all have skulls and backbones. Discuss the differences in the shapes of the skeletons and the size of the bones.

3. Look at worms, slugs and snails, which do not have internal skeletons to support them. Notice how they move without bones and joints.

4. Talk about bones being strong and light. Look at different bones whenever you get the chance, for example, cooked chicken, fish and lamb bones. Notice the differences between them and work out which part of the body they come from. (It is best if the bones are handled only by an adult.)

5. Find all the places in your body that bend and name the joints. You could play a game of 'Simon says', changing the instructions to: "Simon says bend your elbow", (or wrist, knee, etc.) Sit down if you bend the wrong joint!

Index